STICKMEN'S GUIDE
TO
SCIENCE

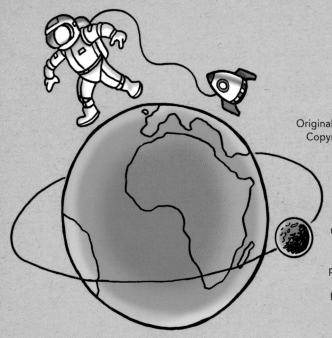

Thanks to the creative team:
Senior Editor: Alice Peebles
Fact Checking: Tom Jackson
Design: Perfect Bound Ltd

Hungry Tomato®
A division of Lerner Publishing Group, Inc.
241 First Avenue North
Minneapolis, MN 55401 USA

For reading levels and more information, look up
this title at www.lernerbooks.com.

Main body text set in Avenir LT Std 9/5/12.
Typeface provided by Linotype AG.

Library of Congress Cataloging-in-Publication Data

Names: Farndon, John, author. | Matthews, Joe,
1963– illustrator.
Title: Stickmen's guide to science / John Farndon ;
[illustrator] Joe Mathews [Matthews].
Description: Minneapolis : Hungry Tomato, [2018] |
Series: Stickmen's guides to STEM | Audience: Ages
8–12. | Audience: Grades 4 to 6.
Identifiers: LCCN 2018004243 (print) | LCCN
2018010803 (ebook) | ISBN 9781541523937 (eb pdf)
| ISBN 9781541500594 (lb : alk. paper)
Subjects: LCSH: Science—Miscellanea—Juvenile
literature. | Children's questions and answers.
Classification: LCC Q175.2 (ebook) | LCC Q175.2
.F37 2018 (print) | DDC 502—dc23

LC record available at
https://lccn.loc.gov/2018004243

Manufactured in the United States of America
1-43700-33492-4/19/2018

STICKMEN'S GUIDE TO SCIENCE

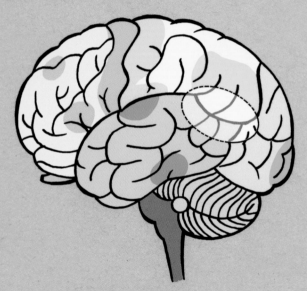

by John Farndon

Illustrated by Joe Matthews

HUNGRY TOMATO®

Minneapolis

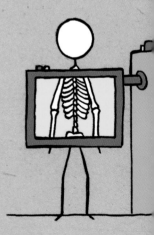

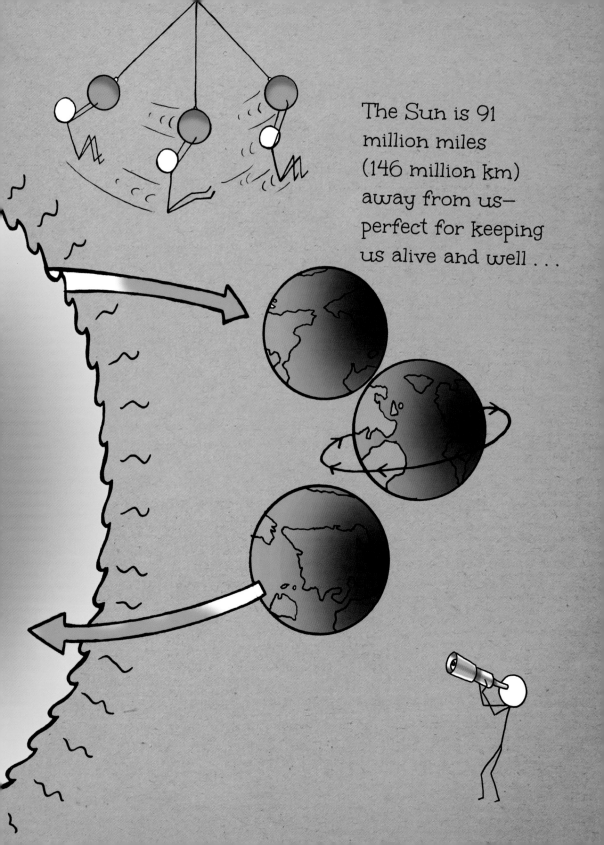

The Sun is 91 million miles (146 million km) away from us—perfect for keeping us alive and well . . .

Contents

About Science

Scientists are people who explore the world and how it works. They study everything from how microbes grow to what happens when a volcano erupts. They look for patterns and rules that help us understand why things happen, and they predict what might happen in the future.

What do scientists do?

Scientists ask questions and then try to answer them with experiments, observations, and mathematical reasoning. Sometimes they work things out on paper. Sometimes they try things out in a laboratory. Sometimes they go out into the world and collect data.

John Dalton (1766–1844) proposed the theory that chemicals are made from different atoms.

Scientific theories

Scientists like theories. Theories are a fully worked out explanation of how something works. But a theory is only any good if it can be tested in the real world and be proven correct. Newton's theory of gravity shows how things fall. Dalton's atomic theory shows how each chemical **element** has its own unique **atom**.

The scientific method

Scientists like to follow what they call the scientific method. First they decide a question to ask, such as why does rain fall. Then they do some basic thinking and research and come up with a first idea of why, called a hypothesis. Finally, they do tests to see if the hypothesis is right. If the tests work, they tell other scientists so they can try it out too.

Science on the rise

There are nearly 8 million scientists at work around the world today. That's more than 90 percent of the scientists who ever lived. The number of scientific research reports written doubles every nine years. So it's not surprising that scientific breakthroughs are being made faster than ever.

Aristotle, one of the forefathers of natural philosophy

Natural philosophers

There are many different kinds of scientists today, each one specializing in a different field. For example, particle physicists study the parts of atoms, and microbiologists study life under a microscope. In the past, though, scientists studied a wide range of subjects and were called "natural philosophers." The term "scientist" was invented in the 1830s.

Things Moving

If nothing moved, the universe would be boring. In fact, it would be dead. It's movement that makes things interesting. That's why physics is the most basic of all sciences. Physics is about movement or, as scientists say, "motion," and it looks at everything from how a football spins to how the universe moves.

Feel the force!

Physicists are very interested in **forces**. Things move because of forces. A force is basically a push or pull. It makes things accelerate—that is, change speed or direction.

1 When a baseball player swings the bat, he transfers the force of his muscles to the bat.

2 When the bat hits the ball, the force of the bat swing is transferred to the ball.

Stop and go

Nothing ever moves without force. Things have what is called **inertia** and move only when a force gives them a start. But once moving, inertia keeps them moving at the same speed and direction, only changing when a force intervenes. This impulse is called **momentum**.

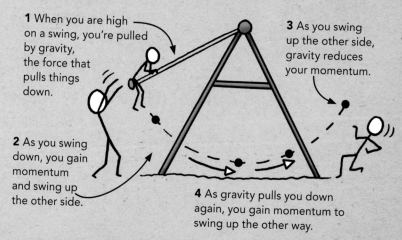

1 When you are high on a swing, you're pulled by gravity, the force that pulls things down.

2 As you swing down, you gain momentum and swing up the other side.

3 As you swing up the other side, gravity reduces your momentum.

4 As gravity pulls you down again, you gain momentum to swing up the other way.

Faster, faster!

"Positive" **acceleration** is when something gets faster. There is also "negative" acceleration—when something slows down. Indeed, physicists call any change in direction acceleration. And any kind of acceleration needs a force.

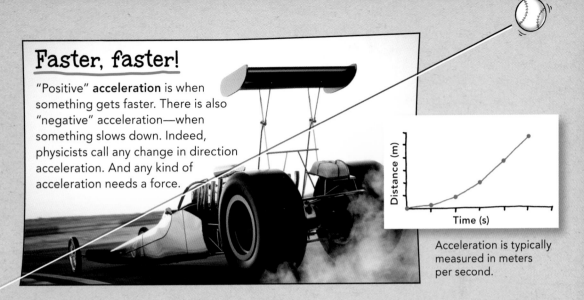

Distance (m) / Time (s)

Acceleration is typically measured in meters per second.

1 When an archer stretches back a bow, she gives the bowstring stored energy.

Energize!

Besides forces, physicists are obsessed with **energy**. Energy is what you need to exert a force or make things happen, usually by heating it or making it move. Physicists call this doing "work." Movement (kinetic) energy is energy in action—the energy that things have when they're moving. Stored (potential) energy is energy that is stored and ready to use.

2 When the archer lets go, the string's energy gives the arrow movement energy as it flies forward.

Changing energy

The amount of energy that exists is always the same. But it can move (transfer) or change from one form to another (transform). It also continually switches between movement energy and stored energy. Your body gets the energy to move by converting the energy stored in food. But once the task is done, the energy isn't lost—it's simply changed to heat.

Stuff Happens

Matter is every substance in the universe—everything that's not just empty space! It can be anything from solid chunks of metal to wispy clouds of gas, but it is all made up from a range of substances called chemicals. The scientists who study chemicals are called chemists.

In a state

Every substance is made of tiny, tiny pieces called **molecules**, which are much, much too small to see! The way these molecules interact means matter comes in three main forms—solid, liquid, and gas. These are called the states of matter. They seem very different, but they can switch from one to the other and back if the temperature and pressure are right.

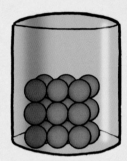 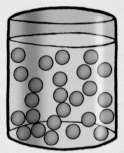 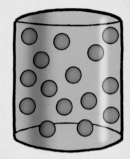

A solid has a definite volume and a definite shape because its molecules are locked together in a regular structure and vibrate on the spot. The hotter it gets, the more they vibrate.

A liquid flows into the shape of any container. This is because the bonds between the molecules are loose enough to slide over each other like grains of dry sand.

A gas has no definite shape or volume, and expands to fit any space. This is because the molecules move so fast that they do not hold together.

Melting and boiling

When substances warm up, the molecules move more and more. So they go from solid to liquid (melting) and from liquid to gas (evaporation). Once the temperature reaches a certain temperature (boiling point), the liquid will get no hotter and simply evaporates.

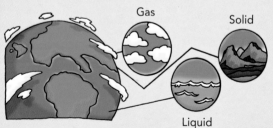

Gas

Solid

Liquid

Condensing and freezing

When substances cool down, the molecules move less. So they change from gas to liquid (condensing) and from liquid to solid (freezing).

Seriously tiny!

Matter and molecules are built up from even tiny atoms. Atoms are so tiny that they can only be seen under very powerful microscopes—and they're not solid balls, just clumps of energy. Nearly every atom has a nucleus, or center, made of two kinds of particles: protons and neutrons. Even tinier particles, called electrons, whiz around the nucleus.

Scientists can see atoms (left) with special microscopes (above).

Mixing it up

All the substances in the universe are made from just 120 or so basic chemicals or elements, such as gold and carbon. Each has its own special character and unique kind of atom. Atoms of different elements can join to form combination chemicals called **compounds**. When substances mingle without joining chemically, it's called a mixture.

Pure chemicals
Element: helium
Compound: water

Mixtures
Varied mixture: wet sand
Uniform mixture: tea with sugar

Impure drinks

Even clean water usually contains tiny, invisible traces of other substances. That's why scientists call it a **solution**. A solution is a liquid with solids dissolved in it. When a solid dissolves, it breaks up and vanishes in the liquid but is still there.

- In a solution, solids are dissolved invisibly
- In a colloid, such as milk, tiny solids are mixed in but not dissolved, making the liquid cloudy
- In a suspension, bigger grains of solids float but will eventually sink

Seeing Stars

The few thousand stars you see in the sky at night are just a tiny fraction of the mega-trillions in the universe—and astronomers would like to study them all! Astronomy is the oldest of all sciences, but it is now making some of the most exciting scientific discoveries of all.

Day and night

To us on Earth, it looks as if the sun is moving through the sky. But it's really Earth moving while the sun stays still. Earth spins around every 24 hours. It turns us to face the sun and then turns us away again, giving us day and night. Earth also goes on a journey around the sun, called its orbit, and this takes a year.

Sun time

The direction of the sun changes steadily during the day, moving from east to west across the sky. It moves so steadily, you can tell the time from the direction of your shadow.

Stars wheeling around the Pole Star, as seen from the Rocky Mountains

Round and round

Earth whirls around the sun along with a small family of planets called the **solar system**. Four small rocky planets, including Earth, orbit close to the sun, and four giant gas planets orbit farther out. Most planets are also circled by their own moons, and in between the planets are lots of lumps called asteroids— and icy chunks called comets that whiz in and out.

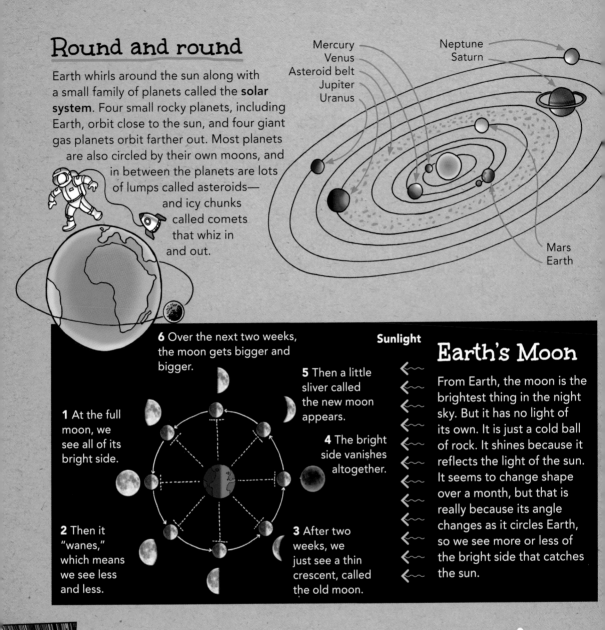

Mercury
Venus
Asteroid belt
Jupiter
Uranus

Neptune
Saturn

Mars
Earth

Earth's Moon

From Earth, the moon is the brightest thing in the night sky. But it has no light of its own. It is just a cold ball of rock. It shines because it reflects the light of the sun. It seems to change shape over a month, but that is really because its angle changes as it circles Earth, so we see more or less of the bright side that catches the sun.

Sunlight

1 At the full moon, we see all of its bright side.

2 Then it "wanes," which means we see less and less.

3 After two weeks, we just see a thin crescent, called the old moon.

4 The bright side vanishes altogether.

5 Then a little sliver called the new moon appears.

6 Over the next two weeks, the moon gets bigger and bigger.

Steering by the stars

As Earth turns, the stars seem to wheel slowly through the sky. In fact, they stay in the same place. But in the northern half of the world, there is one bright star, right in the middle of the wheel, which never moves. It is called the North Star or Pole Star, and in olden days sailors used it to show them which way north is.

You can find the Pole Star by looking for a distinctive group of stars called the Big Dipper, which points to it.

The Deep Blue Sea

Nearly three-quarters of the world is covered by five great oceans: the Pacific, Atlantic, Indian, Southern, and Arctic. They are so deep and dark that we know only a little about them. But scientists who study oceans (oceanographers) are discovering more and more.

Making waves

Ocean waves begin far out in the ocean, as winds blow the surface into ripples. The ripples pile up into waves called swell. The water in waves barely moves, just rolling around as waves swell up and passing on their energy to the next wave. But as they near the coast, waves pile up and spill over to "break" onto the shore in an avalanche of foam.

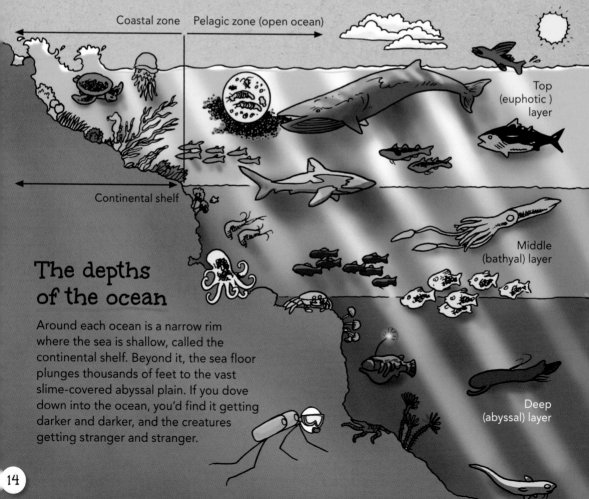

Coastal zone | Pelagic zone (open ocean)

Top (euphotic) layer

Continental shelf

Middle (bathyal) layer

The depths of the ocean

Around each ocean is a narrow rim where the sea is shallow, called the continental shelf. Beyond it, the sea floor plunges thousands of feet to the vast slime-covered abyssal plain. If you dove down into the ocean, you'd find it getting darker and darker, and the creatures getting stranger and stranger.

Deep (abyssal) layer

Deep pressure

As you go deeper into the ocean, the water squeezes harder. Submarines can go down about 0.6 miles (1 km) before the pressure begins to crush them. You can see how pressure increases with depth with a plastic bottle or cardboard carton.

1 Make three equal sized holes in the carton, one at the top, one in the middle and one at the bottom. Tape over the holes with sticky tape.

2 Place the carton in a basin. Fill it with water, then pull the sticky tape off quickly to open the holes.

3 See how the water squirts out much farther from the bottom hole because of the greater pressure.

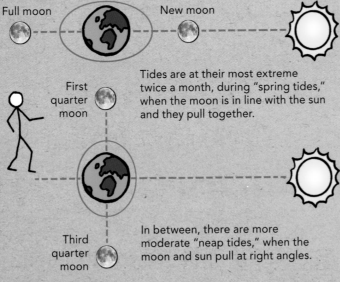

Full moon   New moon

First quarter moon

Third quarter moon

Tides are at their most extreme twice a month, during "spring tides," when the moon is in line with the sun and they pull together.

In between, there are more moderate "neap tides," when the moon and sun pull at right angles.

Tide up

Tides are the rise and fall of the sea that happens twice every day. They are caused by the pull of gravity between Earth and the moon. This stretches the ocean out in line with the moon, so there is one high tide on the side of Earth nearest the moon and another on the far side. This tidal bulge moves around Earth as it turns, bringing high tides twice daily.

Why is the sea salty?

The sea is salty because rivers carry the salty parts of dissolved rock into the sea. Over time, enough salt has washed into the sea to cover the entire world in salt to a depth of 500 feet (150 m)!

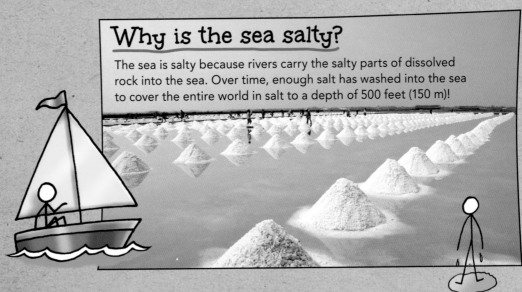

You're My World

We humans have been living on Earth a long, long time. But it's only in recent years that earth scientists and geologists (rock scientists) have begun to discover how its landscapes are shaped, and how it's all put together.

World on a plate

Earth's surface is cracked into giant slabs of rock called tectonic plates that are forever shifting around the world, carrying the continents with them. There are seven gigantic plates, ten smaller plates, and dozens of "micro" plates.

The biggest plate is the Pacific Plate under the Pacific Ocean.

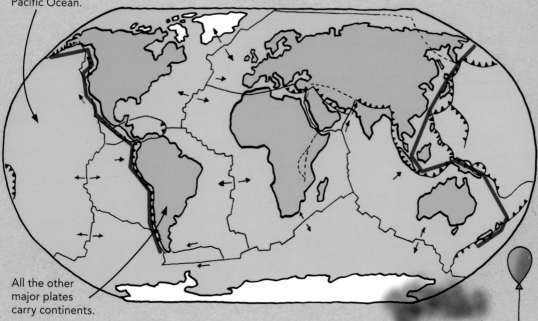

All the other major plates carry continents.

Hot mountains

Volcanoes are places where red-hot liquid rock (magma) from the mantle bursts onto the surface. Sometimes the magma oozes out slowly. Sometimes it explodes, blasting out ash, gases, and lava. The world's 500 or so active volcanoes lie mostly along the cracks between tectonic plates, especially in a "Ring of Fire" (in red on the map above) around the Pacific Ocean.

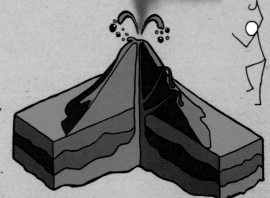

What's inside?

Earth is a bit like an egg. It has a thin shell of tough rock called the crust; a **mantle** (the egg white) of hot, half-melted rock; and a superhot metal "core" (the yolk) of iron and nickel. The mantle is continually churning about, moving the plates on the surface and setting off volcanoes and earthquakes. The circulation of the metal core makes Earth magnetic.

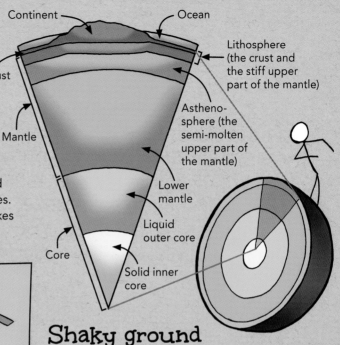

Continent

Ocean

Lithosphere (the crust and the stiff upper part of the mantle)

Crust

Asthenosphere (the semi-molten upper part of the mantle)

Mantle

Lower mantle

Liquid outer core

Core

Solid inner core

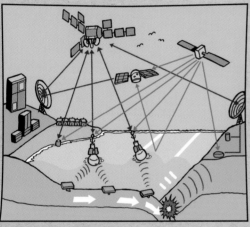

Shaky ground

The worst earthquakes occur in earthquake zones along boundaries between tectonic plates. They are set off when the plates suddenly jolt past each other. The jolt sends shock waves or "seismic waves" through the ground. Earthquake scientists monitor the ground all the time for slight movements showing an earthquake might be on its way.

Make your own weather station

You can make your own weather station to record the changes in weather through the year. The basic equipment can be bought cheaply online. You will need:

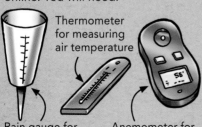

Thermometer for measuring air temperature

Rain gauge for collecting rain

Anemometer for measuring the wind

Something in the air

Meteorologists (weather scientists) study the atmosphere to warn if a storm is on its way. They are helped by satellite pictures that show shifting clouds and by computers that process data from thousands of weather stations on atmospheric conditions, including temperature, moisture content, air pressure, and wind.

That's Life

The variety of life on Earth is amazing, so biologists (scientists who study living things) have a lot to study. Over 1.25 million species of animals, 391,000 plants, and 10,000 microbes are known, and some biologists think there may be trillions we've yet to discover.

Cells are the building blocks of life.

Cells make tissues, such as skin.

Tissues make organs, such as the brain or heart.

Building life

Amazingly, all living things or organisms are made from tiny cells that can only be seen under a microscope. The simplest organisms, such as bacteria, consist of just one cell. More complex creatures are made by lots of different kinds of cells growing together. We humans are made from 37.2 trillion cells!

Animals and plants make communities.

Organs and tissues combine to make animals and plants.

Life packages

All cells have the same basic structure: a thin skin or membrane wrapped around a jelly-like mixture of chemicals called the cytoplasm. This contains various structures called organelles. Plant and animal cells have a control center, or nucleus; bacteria and similar organisms do not.

Plant cells have:

Tough outer wall of cellulose

Organelles called chloroplasts, which trap the sun's energy

Large space filled with air or water called a vacuole

Nucleus

Animal cells have:

Soft membrane with no rigid wall

Tiny vacuoles

Nucleus

Variety of organelles

Animal cells

An animal cell is a tiny chemical factory containing a variety of organelles, each with its own function.

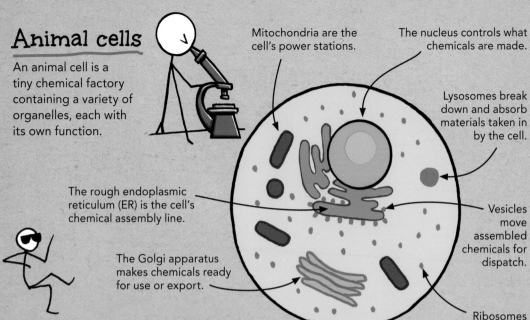

Mitochondria are the cell's power stations.

The nucleus controls what chemicals are made.

Lysosomes break down and absorb materials taken in by the cell.

The rough endoplasmic reticulum (ER) is the cell's chemical assembly line.

Vesicles move assembled chemicals for dispatch.

The Golgi apparatus makes chemicals ready for use or export.

Ribosomes build chemicals.

Animal watching

Botanists study plants and zoologists study animals. Often, zoologists learn about animals by watching them from secret observation points called hides as they go about their lives. Remote control cameras help get good pictures without disturbing the animals.

Growing a bean

Even the biggest, most complex living thing starts small and simple. You can see for yourself how an entire plant grows from just a tiny bean.

1 Roll a piece of blotting paper and slot it inside a jam jar.

2 Slide a bean between the jar and paper, halfway down the jar.

3 Put a few tablespoons of water in the jar and place the jar in a cupboard.

4 After a week, remove the jar from the cupboard. Plant the shoot in a pot of soil and place it on a windowsill.

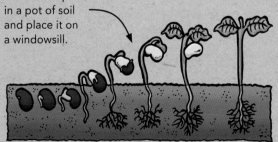

Home Ground

Most plants or animals are very choosy. They have their own natural place, or habitat, in the world and can only live happily there. Their chosen habitat may be the mattress on your bed for a bedbug or the whole of the Arctic for a polar bear.

Natural regions

The world's weather varies from the bitter chill of the polar regions to the scorching heat of tropical deserts. The typical weather in a place is called its climate. Different climates create natural regions called **biomes**, each home to its own unique range of plants and animals, such as those shown in the diagram. The oceans are the biggest natural biomes of all.

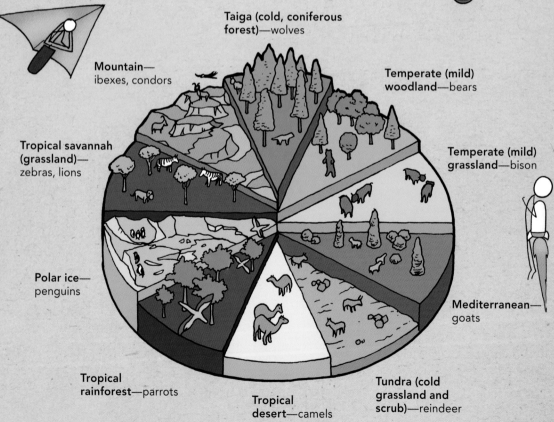

Taiga (cold, coniferous forest)—wolves

Mountain—ibexes, condors

Temperate (mild) woodland—bears

Tropical savannah (grassland)—zebras, lions

Temperate (mild) grassland—bison

Polar ice—penguins

Mediterranean—goats

Tropical rainforest—parrots

Tropical desert—camels

Tundra (cold grassland and scrub)—reindeer

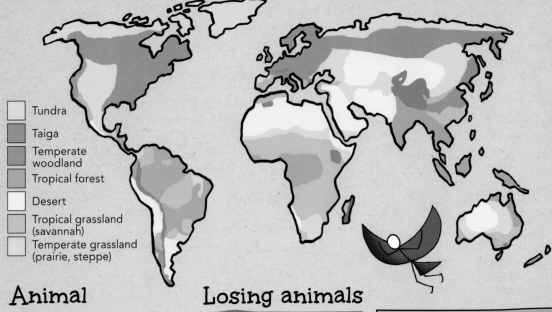

- Tundra
- Taiga
- Temperate woodland
- Tropical forest
- Desert
- Tropical grassland (savannah)
- Temperate grassland (prairie, steppe)

Animal homes

Each continent has a range of biomes, except for Antarctica, which is entirely within the polar biome.

Life systems

Plants and animals survive by living together in interacting communities called **ecosystems**. They pass around vital substances, such as carbon, oxygen, and water. They provide food for each other, and the way that plants and animals are linked together by eating each other is called a food chain.

Plants such as trees are "producers" because they can make their own food from sunlight.

Losing animals

Human activity is now so intense, with expanding cities and increased pollution and demands for food and produce, that natural habitats like rainforests are being destroyed rapidly. As a result, many animal species are in danger of dying out, including such wonderful animals as polar bears and rhinos. Some experts predict that more than a third of all species will be lost in the next 40 years.

"Consumers" eat other living things for food.

"Primary" consumers such as rabbits eat producers (plants).

"Secondary" consumers eat primary consumers, like foxes eat rabbits.

"Decomposers" in the soil, such as bacteria and fungi, break down the remains of living things, such as fallen leaves.

Life Matters

Living things only live a short while. But their kind lives on because they reproduce, or make copies of themselves. Plants make seeds from which new plants grow. Animals have babies.

The instruction book

Inside every living cell is a remarkable spiral-shaped molecule called **DNA**. DNA contains all the instructions the cell needs to live, and all the instructions to make an exact copy of itself. Like a computer, DNA carries instructions in code. The code is given by the order in which simple chemicals called bases are arranged.

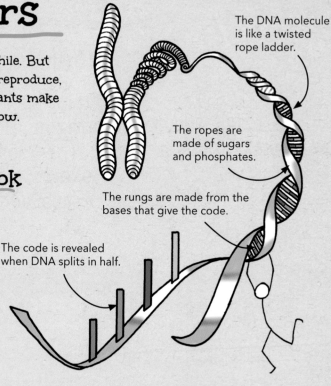

The DNA molecule is like a twisted rope ladder.

The ropes are made of sugars and phosphates.

The rungs are made from the bases that give the code.

The code is revealed when DNA splits in half.

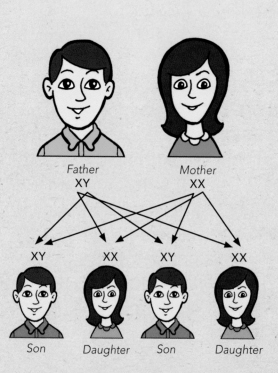

Father
XY

Mother
XX

XY

XX

XY

XX

Son

Daughter

Son

Daughter

Who's a male and who's a female?

Our DNA is packaged in 46 bundles called chromosomes. Typically, girls have 23 matching pairs and boys have 22 plus two odd ones: one X-shaped, the other Y-shaped. Most girls have two X chromosomes; most boys an X and a Y. A dad's XY and a mom's XX mix and match so they can have boys or girls as children. Other mixes (like XYY) are rare but possible.

Genes

The DNA code is arranged in genes. Each gene is instructions for a particular feature in your body. You get one set from your mom and one from your dad. With some features, the two work together. With others, either your mom's or dad's wins out. A gene that always wins, like the gene for brown eyes, is a "dominant" gene; one that loses is a "recessive" gene. A recessive gene will win if paired with the same gene.

Flower colors

In this diagram, each flower shares its genes for color with another flower to pass on to the next generation. Purple is a dominant gene and white recessive. Only when there is no purple gene will the flower actually turn out white.

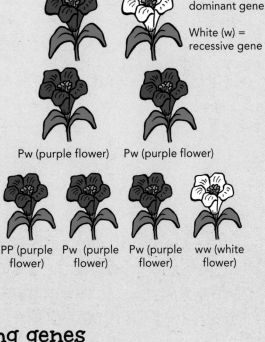

Purple (P) = dominant gene

White (w) = recessive gene

Pw (purple flower)   Pw (purple flower)

PP (purple flower)   Pw (purple flower)   Pw (purple flower)   ww (white flower)

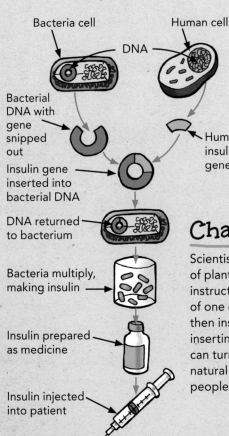

Bacteria cell

Human cell

DNA

Bacterial DNA with gene snipped out

Human insulin gene

Insulin gene inserted into bacterial DNA

DNA returned to bacterium

Bacteria multiply, making insulin

Insulin prepared as medicine

Insulin injected into patient

Changing genes

Scientists have learned how to alter the genes of plants and animals to give them different life instructions. They snip the gene from the DNA of one organism using biological scissors. They then insert this into the other organism. By inserting a gene in the DNA of bacteria, they can turn the bacteria into factories for making natural chemicals, such as insulin for treating people who have the disease diabetes.

Your Body

Some are big. Some are small. Some are tall. Some are short. But all our bodies work in the same way. The study of body processes is called physiology, and the study of the way the body is put together is called anatomy.

Body systems

The body is made up of a range of interlocking systems, each with a particular task. Some extend through the whole body, like the skeleton, muscles, and nerves. Others, like digestion, are localized.

Whole systems

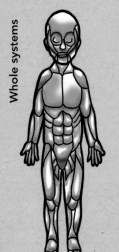
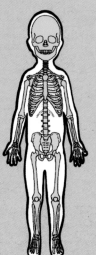

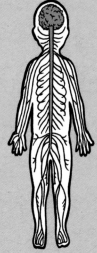

Your muscles enable you to move.

Your skeleton, or framework of bones, supports your body and protects organs.

Your heart and blood circulation supply body cells with oxygen and food.

Your nervous system is the brain and nerves that sense the world and control your body.

Your lymphatic system carries fluid that helps fight disease and clean out waste.

Local systems

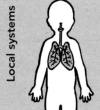

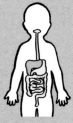

Respiratory (breathing) system

Hormone (chemical message) system

Digestive system

Excretory (waste) system

Cell-making machine

Your body is an amazing, around-the-clock, cell-making machine. Every moment of your life, it's making millions of new cells as old ones die. That's how you stay alive and healthy—and it's how you grow. Before you're born, you have special cells that can split to form any kind of cell. Later, most cells are specialized.

Your life begins with stem cells

Blastocysts (new baby cells)

Stem cells, from which other cells can grow

Red blood cells

Nerve cells

Heart muscle cells

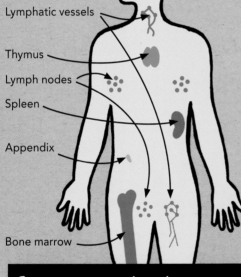

Tonsils

Lymphatic vessels

Thymus

Lymph nodes

Spleen

Appendix

Bone marrow

Fighting illness

Every now and then, your body comes under attack from germs, such as bacteria and viruses, that cause disease. Fortunately, it has an array of clever defenses to deal with them if they ever get in. At the heart of this is the lymphatic system and an array of special cells called lymphocytes, made in certain places around the body.

Looking into it

In the past, scientists found out about the body mostly by cutting into corpses. Now they can see inside living bodies with an array of imaging devices, such as X-rays, MRI scans, PET scans, and CT scans. These penetrate the body with invisible rays to take pictures of what's going on inside.

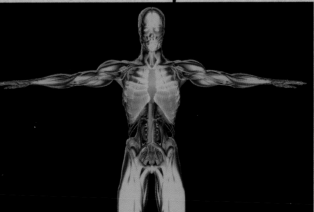

Mind You

Your head contains the most amazing structure in the universe: the human brain. It's packed with an incredible network of nerve connections that enable you to think and control your body. Scientists who study it are called psychologists.

Brain map

The outside of your brain, or cortex, is where conscious thoughts go on, and its folds allow a lot to be packed in. Lots of thoughts seem to take up the whole of your brain. Yet certain places in the brain, called association areas, seem to become especially active when you're doing certain things.

Frontal lobe: where you decide what to do and where to move

Parietal lobe: sensing things, being aware, paying attention, reading

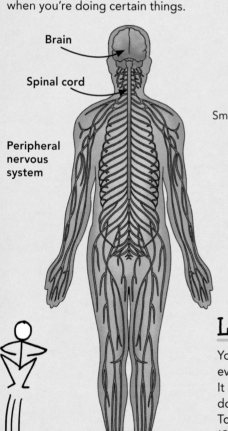

Brain

Spinal cord

Peripheral nervous system

Smell

Hearing

Temporal lobe: imagination, cleverness and emotion, language

Occipital lobe: processing what you see

Lots of nerve

Your nervous system is like a busy internet, wired to every part of your body, whizzing messages to and fro. It centers on your brain and a bundle of nerves running down through your backbone, called the spinal cord. Together, they're known as the central nervous system (CNS). From the CNS, nerves branch out to the whole body to form the peripheral nervous system (PNS).

In and out

Nerves are the connections between your brain and your body. Sensory nerves send the brain messages from sensors in your body such as ears, which detect sounds, and nerve ends in your skin, which react to touch. Motor nerves go out from your brain telling muscles to move.

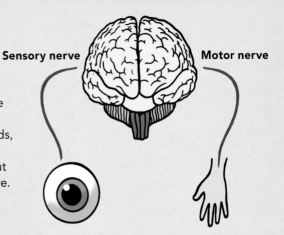

Sensory nerve   Motor nerve

Remember, remember

Your brain creates memories by making new connections between brain cells in three stages.

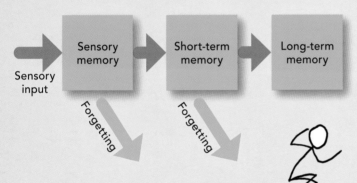

Sensory input

Sensory memory → Short-term memory → Long-term memory

Forgetting   Forgetting

1 Sensory memory: your senses go on seeing, hearing, or feeling something a short while after it stops.

2 Short-term memory: your brain stores something like a name just long enough to pass it on.

3 Long-term memory: your brain makes strong connections so that you remember things for a long time.

Memories for keeps

Some memories fade quickly, but psychologists have found your brain keeps memories longer in various ways.

Your brain learns some things only by repeated practice, such as playing football or the piano. This is called implicit memory.

Other things you learn more quickly, such as people's names or facts for school. This is called semantic memory.

Still other memories are formed by individual dramatic incidents. This is called episodic memory.

Timeline of Science

Human beings are very curious and always making scientific discoveries. There are key breakthroughs being made right now! Here's a rundown of a few of the most famous and important discoveries through history.

220 BCE
Greek thinker Archimedes proved with math that the power of a lever to move a load depends on how far from the fulcrum you apply your effort.

1543
Polish astronomer Copernicus showed for the first time that Earth is moving all the time and circles the sun. But for a while, most people thought he was nuts.

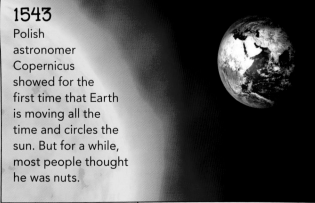

200 BCE   **1500**   **1600**

c.830 CE
In Baghdad, super clever Persian Jabir ibn Hayyan (Geber) gave the world the chemistry lab. He discovered distillation and acids strong enough to dissolve metals!

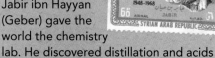

1543
In Italy, Vesalius made the first complete maps of the human body by cutting up dead bodies. This is called anatomy. You might call it butchery.

1610
Italian science whiz Galileo made a telescope for looking at the night sky—and proved Copernicus right from the way shadows move on Venus. He did many other clever things too, including showing that things go steadily faster and faster as they fall.

1628
British doctor William Harvey showed that the heart is a pump and continually circulates blood around the body through pipes called arteries and veins. Beat that.

1687

Isaac Newton realized that every movement in the universe obeys three simple mathematical rules, known as the Laws of Motion. He also discovered gravity. And we fell for it.

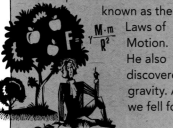

$$F = \gamma \frac{M \cdot m}{R^2}$$

1803

English chemist John Dalton realized that chemical elements are made from solid particles called atoms. Each element is made from atoms of a particular weight. Thrilled to pieces!

1820

Danish physicist Hans Øersted discovered that an electric current creates a magnetic field. Michael Faraday and Joseph Henry used this to create electric motors and electricity generators. Bright sparks!

1780s

Anton Lavoisier made many brilliant discoveries about chemicals and developed the idea of chemical formulas. But he got his head chopped off in the French revolution.

1700   1800   1900

1859

Charles Darwin showed that every species of living thing evolved entirely by "natural selection," as organisms born with differences that help are more likely to survive and have offspring. Life changing!

1911

New Zealand scientist Ernest Rutherford discovered that atoms are mostly empty space but have a dense core of nucleus. He was thrilled to even smaller pieces than Dalton.

1905

Fuzzy-haired super-genius Albert Einstein discovered that time depends on where you are and how fast you're moving. He called this relativity. His relatives couldn't understand it.

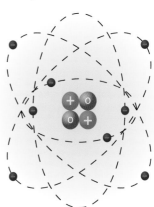

Eureka!

Naked scientist

One day 2,300 years ago, Archimedes was in his bath wondering how to test if the king's crown was pure gold. Then he noticed the water rising and falling—and at once saw the answer. He could test the crown's density by immersing it in water. They say he was so excited that he jumped out of the bath and ran stark naked through the streets to the king shouting, "Eureka!"

Time to swing

One day in 1688, Galileo was in church when he noticed a lamp swinging steadily on a chain. He realized that no matter how high it swung, it always took the same time to swing back and forth. Indeed, when weights swing on a line, they swing so steadily that they can be used to mark time. Galileo had discovered the pendulum, which was used to make the first accurate clocks.

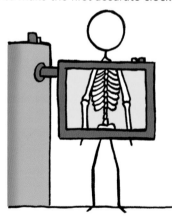

X-rays

One night in 1895, Wilhelm Röntgen shined a glowing electronic tube at his wife's hand with some photographic paper behind. Amazingly, the photo recorded only the bones. The mysterious glowing rays from the tube, which he called X-rays, were shining right through the flesh of his wife's hand to reveal the bones inside. X-rays are now widely used by hospitals.

Slow light

Light is supposed to be the fastest thing in the universe. But one day in 1999, Danish scientist Lene Vestergaard Hau and her team managed to make it travel slower than a bicycle. The next year they stopped it altogether! Their secret was to shine the light through sodium atoms in a special, very cold state, which puts a brake on the photons.

Apple drops

One late summer day in 1666, Isaac Newton was sitting in his garden in Lincolnshire, when he saw an apple drop from a tree. As he watched, he wondered if it wasn't simply falling. Maybe it was being pulled toward the Earth by an invisible force. What if the same invisible force held the moon and the planets in place? He called this force gravity.

Glossary

acceleration: when something changes speed or direction, typically measured in meters per second

atom: the smallest bit of any chemical element

biome: a vast natural region where the climate is similar

compound: a chemical combination of two or more elements

DNA: the special molecule stored inside each living cell that carries the instructions for life as a chemical code

ecosystem: interacting community of living things

element: the simplest, most basic form of chemical, each with its own unique atom

energy: what is needed to exert a force or make things happen, typically by heating it or making it move

force: a push or pull that makes things accelerate; that is, change speed or direction

gene: the instructions for your body to make a particular set of proteins

inertia: the tendency for every mass to stay still or keep moving at the same speed unless forced to change

mantle: the hot, thick middle layer of the earth, beneath the thin crust

molecule: the smallest bit of any substance that can exist by itself

momentum: how much a moving mass wants to keep moving; the faster it's going and the more mass it has, the greater its momentum

solar system: the planets and all the other objects that circle the sun

solution: a liquid in which a solid chemical is so finely spread that the liquid stays liquid

Index

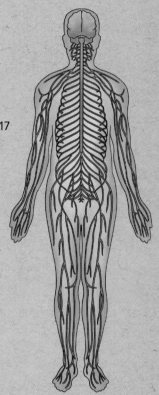

The Author

John Farndon is Royal Literary Fellow at City & Guilds in London, UK, and the author of a huge number of books for adults and children on science, technology, and history, including such international best-sellers as *Do Not Open* and *Do You Think You're Clever?* He has been shortlisted six times for the Royal Society's Young People's Book Prize, for titles such as *How the Earth Works* and *What Happens When?*

The Illustrator

Self-taught comic artist Joe Matthews drew Ivy The Terrible, Ball Boy, and Billy Whizz stories for the *Beano* before moving on to *Tom and Jerry* and *Baby Looney Tunes* comics. He also worked as a storyboard artist on the BBC TV series *Bob the Builder*. Joe has produced his own *Funny Monsters Comic* and in 2016 published his comic-strip version of the Charles Dickens favorite, *A Christmas Carol*. Joe lives in North Wales, UK, with his wife.

Picture Credits

t = top, m = middle, b = bottom, l = left, r = right.

Shutterstock: 11tl; 11tr; Anatomy Insider 25br; Anna_Pushkareva 7tr; AntonSokolov 12br; Bo1982 6ml; chromatos 29br; Digital Storm 9tl; Dragon Images 23tl; dmitry mokshin 29tl; Eugene Ivanov 28mr; Everett Historical 6bl, 28bl, 29m; Georgios Kollidas 29tr; goodluz 6mr; Gorodenkoff 7ml; halitomer 28tl; LightField Studios 11br; Michelangelus 28tr; Morphart Creation 29mr; niall dunne 19ml; Olga Popova 28ml; Ondrej Prosicky 21mr; Panos Karas 7br; Pictureguy 17br; Sarun T 15br; spatuletail 29bl; YANGCHAO 28br.